This book belongs to:

_____

For Winston,
wonderful nephew and word wizard
—Ant (aunt) April

For Lois,
who could never bug anybody
—T. P.

The illustrations were created digitally on a Macintosh using Fractal Design's Painter
The text and display type were set in FanfareJF, Randumhouse and Girls Are Weird
Composed in the United State of America
Art directed and designed by Lois A. Rainwater
Edited by Kristen McCurry

Text © 2005 by April Pulley Sayre
Illustrations © 2005 by Trip Park

NorthWord
Books for Young Readers
11571 K-Tel Drive
Minnetonka, MN 55343
www.tnkidsbooks.com

Library of Congress Cataloging-in-Publication Data

Sayre, April Pulley.
Ant, ant, ant! : an insect chant / by April Pulley Sayre ; illustrated by Trip Park.
p. cm.
ISBN 1-55971-922-2 (hardcover)
1. Insects--Juvenile literature. I. Park, Trip, ill. II. Title.

QL467.2.S29 2005
595.7--dc22
2004031122

Printed in China
10 9 8 7 6 5 4 3 2 1

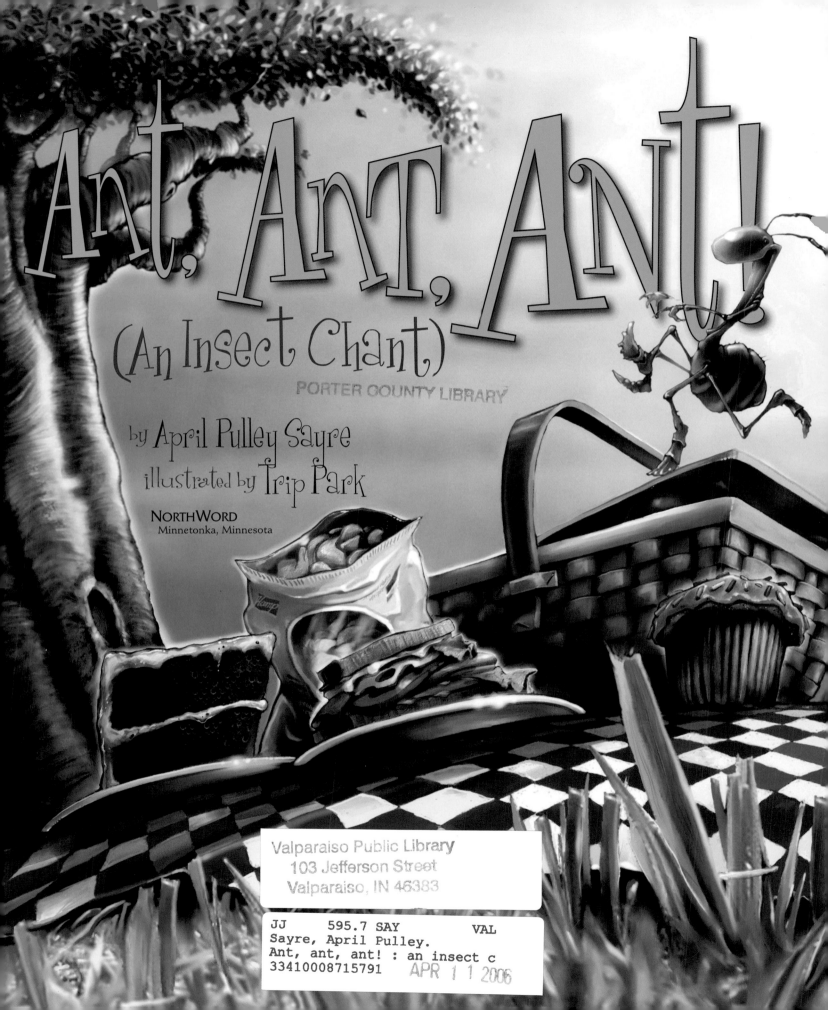

Ant, Ant, Ant!

(An Insect Chant)

by April Pulley Sayre

illustrated by Trip Park

NORTHWORD
Minnetonka, Minnesota

Brush-footed Butterfly,

Leaf-footed Bug,

Bird Dropping Caterpillar,   Slug,
Slug,
Slug!

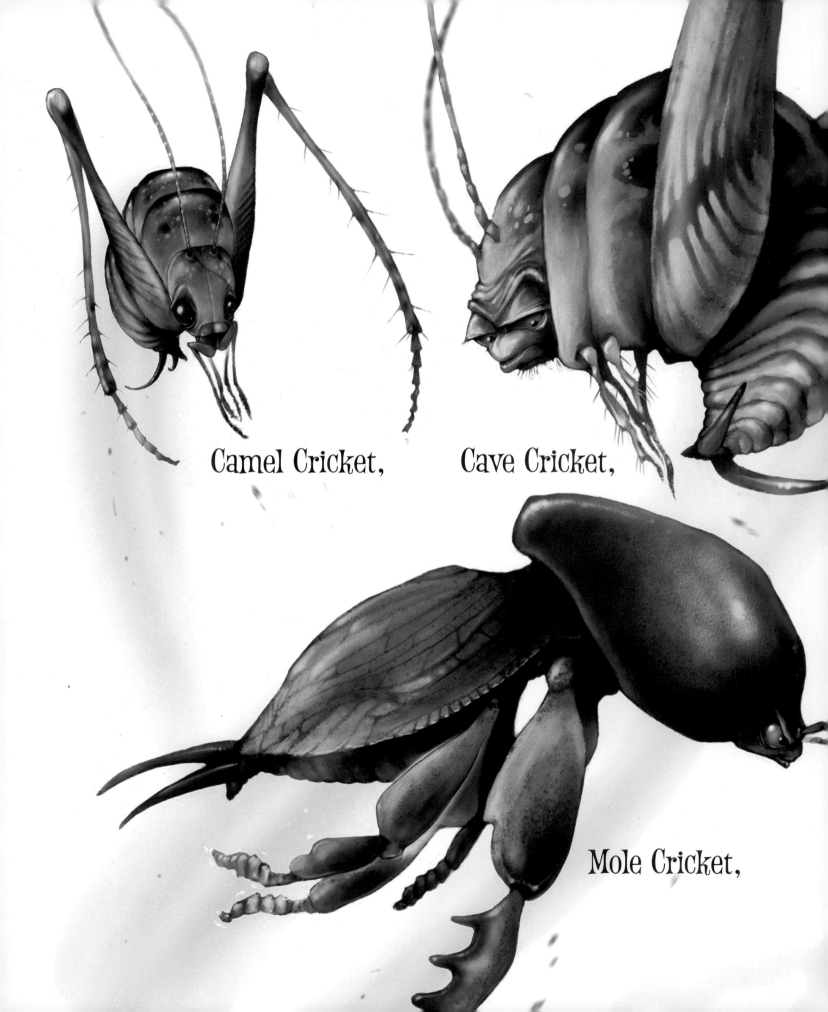

Camel Cricket, Cave Cricket, Mole Cricket,

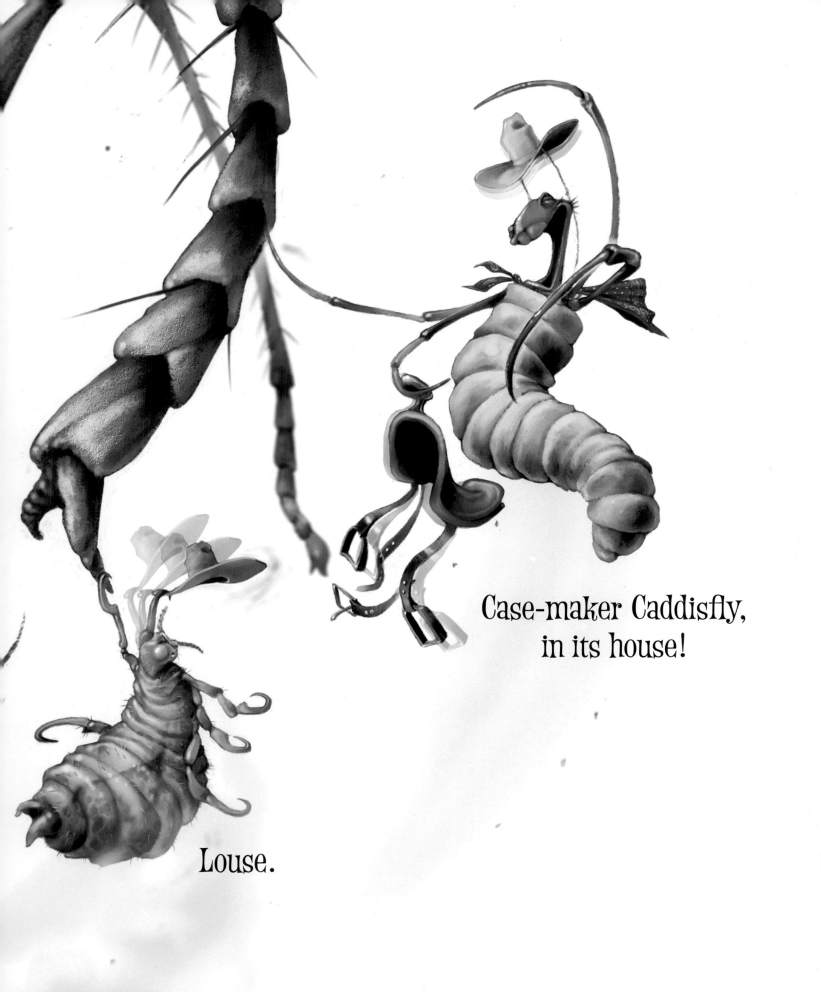

Louse.

Case-maker Caddisfly,
in its house!

Billbug, Bed Bug, Bark Beetle,

Bee.

Flea,
Flea,
Flea!

Painted Lady Butterfly.

Two-spotted Stinkbug,   White-lined Sphinx.

Tiger Moth,

Underwing,
hiding pinks.

Firefly,

Flower Fly,

Ant,
Ant,
Ant!

June Beetle,

May Beetle,

Click.

Corn Beetle,

Walking Stick!

Water Strider,

Woolly Bear,

Luna Moth,   Io Moth,

Sulphur,   Blue.   Housefly,   Black Fly.
Shoo,
shoo,
shoo!

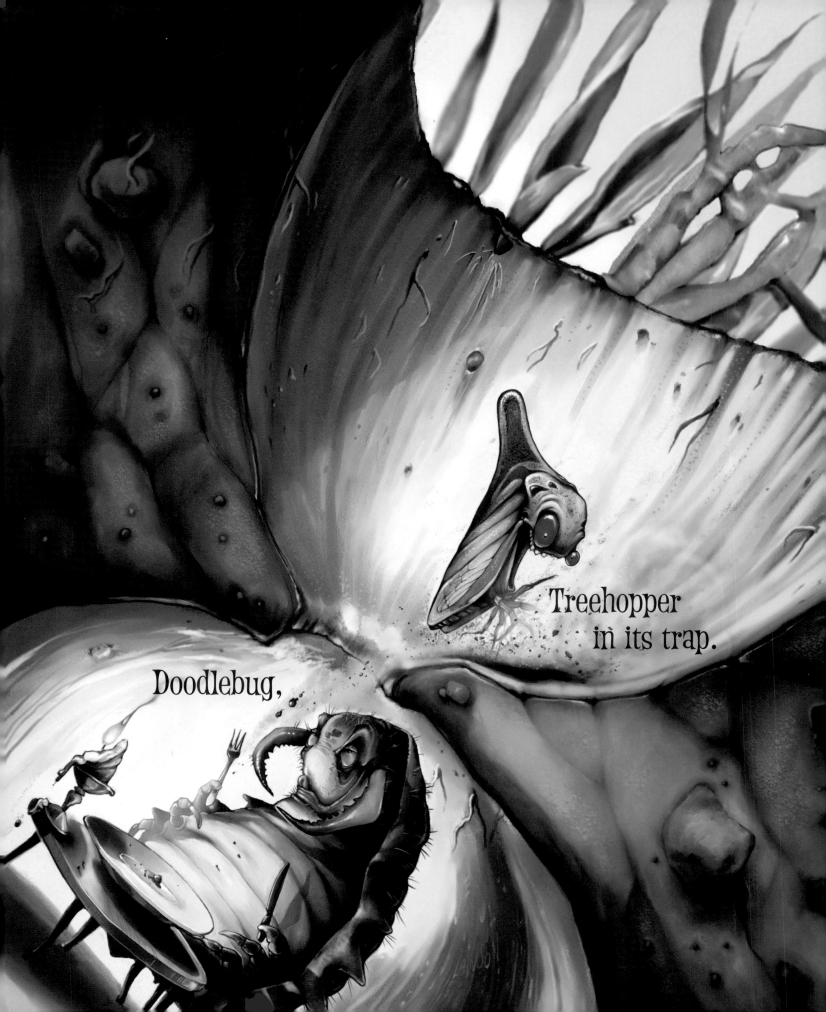

Treehopper
in its trap.

Doodlebug,

Still more beetles:

Sap!

Seed,

Stag,

Conehead,

Dung Beetle, crazy green!

Shadowdragon, Swallowtail,

Queen,
Queen,
Queen!

Grass Moth,

Gold Moth,

Fairy Moth,

Fern.   Lots more moths
for me to learn.

Backswimmer,
Boatman.

Thrips, Thrips, Thrips!

I love insects!
Shout it out!

Hooray for American Insects!

Next time you eat blackberries, tomatoes, or peaches, thank the insects. They pollinate many crops we eat. Insects perform other free "services" too. Ants spread the seeds of woodland wildflowers. Beetle grubs bury dung, fly maggots eat animal carcasses, and termites break down fallen trees. Without this clean-up crew, North America would be a mess!

Of course, some insects feed on people, too! But don't use a glowing insect zapper to kill the mosquitoes—it also kills the insects that eat mosquitoes. However you feel about insects, it won't hurt to get to know the over 87,000 insect species that live in the United States and Canada. Scientists are still identifying new ones. Maybe you'll discover a new species in your backyard!

BRUSH-FOOTED BUTTERFLY

Monarchs and others in the brush-footed butterfly family look as if they have only four legs, because their front two legs are brush-like, tiny, and hard to see.

LEAF-FOOTED BUG

This plant-juice-drinking insect has camouflaged back legs, which are brown and flattened like leaves. In defense, these bugs give off a stinky smell.

BIRD DROPPING CATERPILLAR

The bird dropping caterpillar looks like—what else?—a bird dropping. This camouflage probably helps it avoid being eaten.

SLUG

Slug caterpillars, such as the saddleback caterpillar pictured, vary in body shape. Some look like real slugs, which are the slimy, shell-less relatives of snails.

CAMEL CRICKET

These wingless, humpbacked crickets crawl into basements or other wet, dark places where they scavenge dead insects. Some lay their eggs in bat droppings.

CAVE CRICKET

Cave crickets live in caves but emerge at night to feed on fungi, leaves, fruit, and dead insects.

MOLE CRICKET

With their thick legs, mole crickets burrow into the ground near marshes, streams, and ponds.

LOUSE

Louse is the singular form of the word lice. Lice are small, wingless insects of many species, such as bird lice, hog lice, and human head lice.

CASE-MAKER CADDISFLY

Adult caddisflies look like moths and lay their eggs in water. The larvae—a favorite trout food—protect themselves by wrapping up in silk, sand, twigs, and leaves.

BILLBUG

Billbugs belong to the family *Curculionidae,* which includes the snout beetles and weevils.

BED BUG

Bed bugs infest bat roosts, attics, and bedrooms. These flat, wingless, oval bugs suck mammal blood.

BARK BEETLE

Bark beetles, also called engraver beetles, bore into tree bark, creating tunnels. Different species have different tunnel patterns.

BEE

Bee is a general term for members of superfamily *Apoidea*, which includes seven families of insects. Bees feed on flower nectar and pollen.

PAINTED LADY BUTTERFLY

The painted lady is one of the most widespread butterflies on Earth. It lives in North America, South America, Europe, Africa, and Asia.

FLEA

Fleas are tiny, wingless insects that feed on mammal blood. They can survive without food for weeks until another host comes along.

TWO-SPOTTED STINKBUG

These bugs squeeze out a stinky liquid if disturbed. Two-spotted stinkbugs help farmers by eating crop pests.

WHITE-LINED SPHINX

Sphinx moths hover like hummingbirds and are often mistaken for them. These nectar-eaters can smell flowers from miles away.

TIGER MOTH

The bright colors of tiger moths may warn predators that these moths are full of toxic chemicals and are bad to eat.

UNDERWING MOTH

Underwing moths are named for the colorful patterns on their hindwings. Some underwing caterpillars look like twigs.

COCKROACH

North America has almost 60 kinds of cockroaches. There are 3,500 species worldwide.

EARWIG

Earwigs don't hide in ears or wigs. These nocturnal plant-eaters hide in leaves, bark, and other crevices during the day. They pinch attackers with their two cerci or give off a stinky-smelling liquid.

FIREFLY

Fireflies aren't flies. They're beetles with bioluminescent organs in their abdomens. They flash at night to attract mates. There are many species.

FLOWER FLY

Flower flies, which are flies, are important pollinators. They feed on pollen and nectar.

ANT

Scientists recently found an ant in a 92-million-year-old piece of amber in New Jersey. So ants were here long before people!

MAY (OR JUNE) BEETLE

These brown beetles are attracted to lights at night during May or June. These members of the genus *Phyllophaga* are sometimes called June beetles.

JUNE BEETLE

Confused? If you are, it's for good reason. There's another June beetle, the green June beetle, of the genus *Cotinus*. This kind of muddle often occurs with common names, so scientists agree on one international scientific name for each species. Common names vary from place to place and often overlap. The green June beetles are noisy, buzzing fliers that are active in June or July.

CORN BEETLE

The corn beetle, also called the corn billbug, feeds on grains such as corn.

CLICK BEETLE

Click beetles have a special spine on their thorax that helps them turn over when they are stuck on their back. As they pop upright, they make a clicking sound that helps scare off predators.

More American Insects!

WOOLLY BEAR

The woolly bear is the caterpillar stage of the Isabella tiger moth. As the caterpillar grows, it sheds. With each molt, the size of its red and black segments changes.

WATER STRIDER

Water striders walk on water. They hunt mosquito larvae and other small insects that live in or fall into the water.

WALKING STICK

These well-camouflaged insects do look like sticks. That hides them from birds, which hunt and eat them. Walking sticks eat tree leaves.

LUNA MOTH

Luna moths are large, pale green moths. The caterpillar is bright green with yellow stripes and red dots.

IO MOTH

The bright green caterpillars of these moths have stinging hairs, so don't touch them!

SULPHUR BUTTERFLY

Sulphur butterflies are the yellow color of the mineral sulphur. Some sulphur caterpillars feed on clover.

BLUE BUTTERFLY

Blues are small bluish butterflies of many species.

HOUSEFLY

Housefly larvae, called maggots, eat rotting food such as garbage, carcasses, or manure. Adult houseflies sponge up and drink liquid from rotting food. They can spread disease.

BLACK FLY

Black flies are tiny, biting flies that are common near streams in forested areas of northern North America. The larvae attach themselves to rocks underwater.

DOODLEBUG

To find a doodlebug, look for pits in the sand near a garden, patio, or driveway. Doodlebugs, also called antlions, sit at the bottom of these pits and wait for other insects to slide down so they can eat them. The doodlebug transforms into a flying insect that looks a lot like a damselfly.

TREEHOPPER

Scientists who put microphones on plant stems have found that some treehoppers make complicated calls that travel through the plant stems.

STAG BEETLE

Male stag beetles have large, pinching jaws that look like the antlers of a stag (male deer). The larvae eat decaying wood. Some adults eat tree sap. In some species, the adults do not eat at all.

SEED WEEVIL

The seed weevil, a kind of beetle, eats seeds such as beans and peas.

SAP BEETLE

Sap beetles not only eat sap but also fruit, vegetables, nectar, and fungi. They also are attracted by sugary soft drinks.

CONEHEAD (Cone-headed Grasshopper)

These insects are named for their head shape. There are multiple species, including the swordbearer conehead and the Nebraska conehead.

DUNG BEETLE

Dung beetles roll a piece of dung into a ball. Then they bury the dung ball and lay eggs on it. The dung beetle larvae eat the manure. Dung beetles help recycle dung and "clean up" grasslands.

SHADOWDRAGON

Shadowdragons are dragonflies that hang out in the shadows. Seven species live in the eastern United States.

SWALLOWTAIL

Swallowtails are some of the largest butterflies in the United States. Their name comes from the long tip on each hindwing.

QUEEN CATERPILLAR

The queen caterpillar, like the monarch caterpillar, feeds on milkweed plants.

GRASS MOTH

Grass moths got their name because they feed on grasses during their caterpillar stage.

GOLD MOTH

Gold moths are named for their iridescent gold wings.

FAIRY MOTH

Fairy moths, of the family *Adelinae,* have extremely long antennae.

FERN MOTH

The caterpillars of fern moths eat ferns.

DAMSELFLY

Damselfy species are usually smaller and more slender than dragonflies. At rest, damselflies hold their wings behind them. Most dragonflies hold their wings out to the side.

DRAGONFLY

Dragonflies catch and eat other insects while in mid-air. They may live several years underwater in their nymph stage. Then they spend only a few months as flying adults.

BACKSWIMMER

Backswimmers swim on their backs. Their legs sweep back and forth like oars.

WATER BOATMAN

These flattened insects also sweep their hindlegs back and forth like oars. Unlike backswimmers, water boatmen swim right-side-up.

THRIPS

Some thrips are as small as the period in this sentence. Many are agricultural pests.

QUESTION MARK BUTTERFLY

Question mark butterflies have a question-mark-like marking—a white crescent and dot—on the underside of each hindwing.

COMMA BUTTERFLY

Comma butterflies have a comma-shaped white mark on the underside of their hindwings. The caterpillars eat elms, willows, birches, and currants.

FRITILLARY BUTTERFLY

At the caterpillar stage, the great spangled fritillary feeds on the leaves of violets.

SNOUT BUTTERFLY

As caterpillars, American snouts feed on hackberry trees. Some years, millions of snout butterflies move northward in large groups.

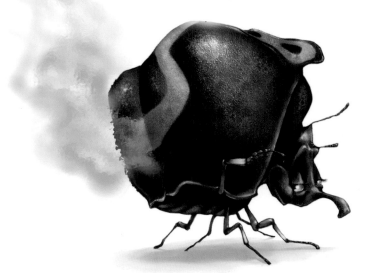

APRIL PULLEY SAYRE is a dragonfly fan and an award-winning author of over 50 books for young readers, including *Trout, Trout, Trout! (A Fish Chant).* Sayre's books, renowned for their lyricism, accuracy, and sometimes silliness, have been translated into French, Dutch, Japanese, and Korean.

Sayre and her husband, Jeff, spend lots of time flitting around the country, sharing the writing process—and the natural world—with school children and educators. For more info, including insect links, go to *aprilsayre.com.*

Most people would run for the repellent when asked to illustrate dozens of insects for the follow-up to *Trout, Trout, Trout! (A Fish Chant).* But TRIP PARK is veritably surrounded by creepy-crawlies on a daily basis with his own four kids. His favorite bug to illustrate from *Ant, Ant, Ant!* would have to be the stinkbug, as he has something very much in common with it...an awfully big smile. You can see more of Trip's scribbles at *tripparkproductions.com.*